# 20 best
# summer drink recipes

**Houghton Mifflin Harcourt**
Boston • New York • 2013

Copyright © 2013 by General Mills, Minneapolis, Minnesota. All rights reserved.

Yoplait is a registered trademark of YOPLAIT MARQUES (France) used under license.

For information about permission to reproduce selections from this book, write to Permissions, Houghton Mifflin Harcourt Publishing Company, 215 Park Avenue South, New York, New York 10003.

www.hmhco.com

Cover photo: Cranberry-Mint Iced Tea (page 10)

### General Mills

Food Content and Relationship Marketing Director: Geoff Johnson
Food Content Marketing Manager: Susan Klobuchar
Senior Editor: Grace Wells
Kitchen Manager: Ann Stuart
Recipe Development and Testing: Betty Crocker Kitchens
Photography: General Mills Photography Studios and Image Library

### Houghton Mifflin Harcourt

Publisher: Natalie Chapman
Editorial Director: Cindy Kitchel
Executive Editor: Anne Ficklen
Associate Editor: Heather Dabah
Managing Editor: Rebecca Springer
Production Editor: Kristi Hart
Cover Design: Chrissy Kurpeski
Book Design: Tai Blanche

ISBN 978-0-544-31486-3
Printed in the United States of America

The Betty Crocker Kitchens seal guarantees success in your kitchen. Every recipe has been tested in America's Most Trusted Kitchens™ to meet our high standards of reliability, easy preparation and great taste.

**FIND MORE GREAT IDEAS AT**
*BettyCrocker*.com

# Dear Friends,

This new collection of colorful mini books has been put together with you in mind because we know that you love great recipes and enjoy cooking and baking but have a busy lifestyle. So every little book in the series contains just 20 recipes for you to treasure and enjoy. Plus, each book is a single subject designed in a bite-size format just for you—it's easy to use and is filled with favorite recipes from the Betty Crocker Kitchens!

All of the books are conveniently divided into short chapters so you can quickly find what you're looking for, and the beautiful photos throughout are sure to entice you into making the delicious recipes. In the series, you'll discover a fabulous array of recipes to spark your interest—from cookies, cupcakes and birthday cakes to party ideas for a variety of occasions. There's grilled foods, potluck favorites and even gluten-free recipes too.

You'll love the variety in these mini books—so pick one or choose them all for your cooking pleasure.

Enjoy and happy cooking!

Sincerely,

*Betty Crocker*

# contents

### Coffee, Tea and Lemonade
Iced Vanilla-Soy Latte • 6
Iced Caramel Cappuccino • 7
Lemon-Ginger Tingler • 8
Watermelon Lemonade • 9
Cranberry-Mint Iced Tea • 10
Chai Iced Tea • 11

### Satisfying Smoothies
Cocoa–Peanut Butter–Banana Smoothies • 12
Granola Berry-Banana Smoothies • 13
Blueberry-Pomegranate Smoothies • 14
Peachy White Tea Smoothies • 15
Creamy Mango Smoothies • 16
Obviously Orange Smoothies • 17
Super-Athlete Spinach Smoothies • 18

### Party Cocktails
Strawberry–Hard Lemonade Slush • 19
Blueberry Hard Lemonade • 20
White Wine Sangria • 21
Skinny Clementine Martini • 22
Thai Basil Mojitarita • 23
Beergaritas • 24
Mango Margaritas • 25

Metric Conversion Guide • 26
Recipe Testing and Calculating Nutrition Information • 27

## Coffee, Tea and Lemonade

# Iced Vanilla-Soy Latte

**Prep Time:** 10 Minutes • **Start to Finish:** 10 Minutes • Makes 2 servings

½ cup ground espresso or French roast coffee

1½ cups water

2 cups vanilla soymilk

2 teaspoons caramel or chocolate fat-free topping

Ice cubes, as desired

Sugar, if desired

Love lattes? Pull off this coffee-shop drink in just a few minutes, using dairy-free soymilk.

**1** Using a drip coffeemaker, brew coffee with water as directed by coffeemaker manufacturer.

**2** In medium bowl, stir together coffee and soymilk. Drizzle topping over inside of each of 2 large glasses.

**3** Fill each glass with ice cubes. Divide soymilk mixture between glasses. Sweeten to taste with sugar.

**1 Serving:** Calories 120; Total Fat 3g (Saturated Fat 0.5g; Trans Fat 0g); Cholesterol 0mg; Sodium 210mg; Total Carbohydrate 16g (Dietary Fiber 0g); Protein 7g **Carbohydrate Choices:** 1

**Tip** Drizzle the topping in interesting designs on the insides of the glasses before filling them.

# Iced Caramel Cappuccino

**Prep Time:** 5 Minutes • **Start to Finish:** 5 Minutes • Makes 4 servings (¾ cup each)

1½ cups water

2 tablespoons instant espresso coffee powder or granules

½ cup caramel topping

2 tablespoons sugar

1 cup milk

½ cup whipped cream topping (from aerosol can)

**1** In 4-cup microwavable measuring cup, microwave water uncovered on High 2 to 3 minutes or until very hot and almost boiling. Stir in coffee powder until dissolved. Stir in ¼ cup of the caramel topping, the sugar and milk.

**2** Fill 4 (12-oz) glasses two-thirds full with ice. Divide coffee mixture among glasses. Top with whipped cream; drizzle with remaining ¼ cup caramel topping.

**1 Serving:** Calories 190; Total Fat 3g (Saturated Fat 2g, Trans Fat 0g); Cholesterol 10mg; Sodium 180mg; Total Carbohydrate 38g (Dietary Fiber 0g); Protein 3g **Carbohydrate Choices:** 2½

**Tip** For a stronger coffee flavor, refrigerate the coffee and caramel mixture until cold before adding the milk and ice. For sweeter coffee, squeeze a bit of caramel topping into the bottom of each glass before filling with ice.

Coffee, Tea and Lemonade • **7**

# Lemon-Ginger Tingler

**Prep Time:** 10 Minutes • **Start to Finish:** 15 Minutes • Makes 6 servings (1 cup each)

1½ cups sugar
1 cup water
1½ cups fresh lemon juice (about 8 lemons)
3 cups ginger ale, chilled
Lemon wedges if desired

**1** In 1-quart saucepan, cook sugar and water over medium heat, stirring constantly, until sugar is dissolved. Remove from heat; cool to room temperature.

**2** Stir in lemon juice.

**3** In each of 6 tall glasses, mix ½ cup chilled juice mixture and ½ cup ginger ale. If desired, add ice. Store juice mixture in tightly covered nonmetal container or jar in refrigerator. Garnish each serving with lemon wedge.

**1 Serving:** Calories 270; Total Fat 0g (Saturated Fat 0g, Trans Fat 0g); Cholesterol 0mg; Sodium 25mg; Total Carbohydrate 66g (Dietary Fiber 0g); Protein 0g **Carbohydrate Choices:** 4½

**Tip** Lemons at room temperature will yield the most juice. You might also want to try warming them a bit in the microwave.

# Watermelon Lemonade

**Prep Time:** 15 Minutes • **Start to Finish:** 1 Hour 15 Minutes • Makes 12 servings (2/3 cup each)

- 3 lb watermelon (without rind), seeded, cut into chunks
- 3 or 4 medium lemons
- 2 medium limes
- 4 cups cold water
- 1 cup sugar
- Watermelon or lemon slices, if desired

**1** In blender, place watermelon. Cover; blend on medium speed about 45 seconds or until smooth. Strain through fine-mesh strainer into 2-quart or larger pitcher.

**2** Squeeze juice from lemons and limes; add to watermelon puree. Stir in cold water and sugar. Refrigerate 1 hour.

**3** Stir before serving. Serve over ice. Garnish with watermelon slice.

**1 Serving:** Calories 120; Total Fat 0g (Saturated Fat 0g, Trans Fat 0g); Cholesterol 0mg; Sodium 0mg; Total Carbohydrate 28g (Dietary Fiber 1g); Protein 1g **Carbohydrate Choices:** 2

**Tip** Honeydew melon balls taste great and add a colorful touch to this crowd-pleasing drink. To make melon balls, use a melon baller to scoop out balls from honeydew melon. Freeze the balls about 1 hour or until frozen. Just before serving, float them in the lemonade.

# Cranberry-Mint Iced Tea

**Prep Time:** 15 Minutes • **Start to Finish:** 25 Minutes • Makes 6 servings (1 cup each)

6 cups cranberry juice cocktail
4 tea bags black tea
10 mint leaves (1 inch each)
2 tablespoons sugar

Chill out with this fresh brewed iced-tea drink, with mint and cranberry juice cocktail. Love mint? Add an extra sprig to each cold glass when serving.

**1** In 2-quart saucepan, heat cranberry juice cocktail to boiling. Pour over tea bags and mint in 2-quart glass measuring cup or heatproof pitcher. Let steep 5 to 10 minutes.

**2** Strain tea mixture through fine mesh strainer. Stir in sugar. Serve over ice. Add more sugar if desired.

**1 Serving:** Calories 160; Total Fat 0g (Saturated Fat 0g, Trans Fat 0g); Cholesterol 0mg; Sodium 5mg; Total Carbohydrate 41g (Dietary Fiber 0g); Protein 0g **Carbohydrate Choices:** 3

**Tip** Be sure to use cranberry juice "cocktail," which contains added sugar, for this refreshing iced tea. Regular cranberry juice is not as sweet and would make this summer sipper much too tart.

# Chai Iced Tea

**Prep Time:** 5 Minutes • **Start to Finish:** 1 Hour 5 Minutes • Makes 6 servings

8 chai tea bags
4 cups hot water
1 tablespoon vanilla
¼ to ½ cup packed brown sugar
½ cup orange-flavored cream soda
½ cup vanilla-flavored cream soda
½ cup milk
6 cinnamon sticks, if desired

**1** Chill 6 glasses in freezer several hours before serving.

**2** Steep tea bags in hot water 3 to 5 minutes. Remove bags. Stir in vanilla and brown sugar until sugar is dissolved. Stir in all remaining ingredients except cinnamon sticks. Refrigerate at least 1 hour to blend flavors.

**3** Serve over ice. Garnish with cinnamon stick.

**1 Serving:** Calories 70; Total Fat 0g (Saturated Fat 0g, Trans Fat 0g); Cholesterol 0mg; Sodium 25mg; Total Carbohydrate 15g (Dietary Fiber 0g); Protein 0g **Carbohydrate Choices:** 1

**Tip** You may want to do a little taste-testing when you add the brown sugar. Depending on the brand of tea used, you might need more or less sugar.

## Satisfying Smoothies

# Cocoa–Peanut Butter–Banana Smoothies

**Prep Time:** 10 Minutes • **Start to Finish:** 10 Minutes • Makes 4 servings (1 cup each)

- 1½ cups Yoplait® 99% Fat Free creamy vanilla yogurt (from 2-lb container)
- 1 cup chocolate milk
- ¼ cup creamy peanut butter
- 2 small bananas, sliced
- 3 to 5 ice cubes
- 1 cup Cocoa Puffs® cereal, coarsely crushed*

**1** Place all ingredients except cereal in blender. Cover; blend on high speed about 30 seconds or until smooth.

**2** Pour into 4 glasses. Sprinkle with cereal. Serve immediately.

**1 Serving:** Calories 310; Total Fat 11g (Saturated Fat 3g, Trans Fat 0g); Cholesterol 10mg; Sodium 190mg; Total Carbohydrate 44g (Dietary Fiber 3g); Protein 10g **Carbohydrate Choices:** 3

*To crush cereal, place in plastic bag or between sheets of waxed paper; crush with rolling pin.*

**Tip** Keep a stash of disposable cups with lids so you can have breakfast on the go or head outside.

# Granola Berry-Banana Smoothies

**Prep Time:** 5 Minutes • **Start to Finish:** 5 Minutes • Makes 2 servings

2 containers (6 oz each) Yoplait Original 99% Fat Free strawberry, mixed berry or red raspberry yogurt

½ cup milk

½ cup fresh strawberry halves or raspberries

1 banana, sliced

2 pouches (1.5 oz each) oats-and-honey crunchy granola bars (4 bars)

**1** In blender, place yogurt, milk, strawberries and bananas. Break up 3 of the granola bars; add to blender. Cover; blend on high speed 10 seconds. Scrape sides.

**2** Cover; blend 20 seconds longer or until smooth.

**3** Pour into 2 glasses. Crumble remaining granola bar; sprinkle in each glass. Serve immediately.

**1 Serving:** Calories 395; Total Fat 10g (Saturated Fat 6g, Trans Fat 0g); Cholesterol 10mg; Sodium 220mg; Total Carbohydrate 70g (Dietary Fiber 5g); Protein 11g **Carbohydrate Choices:** 5½

**Tip** Top each smoothie with fresh strawberries or raspberries.

# Blueberry-Pomegranate Smoothies

**Prep Time:** 5 Minutes • **Start to Finish:** 5 Minutes • Makes 2 servings (¾ cup each)

1 cup frozen blueberries
½ cup pomegranate juice
½ cup soymilk

**1** In blender, place ingredients. Cover; blend on high speed about 1 minute or until smooth.

**2** Pour into 2 glasses. Serve immediately.

**1 Serving:** Calories 140; Total Fat 2g (Saturated Fat 0g, Trans Fat 0g); Cholesterol 0mg; Sodium 40mg; Total Carbohydrate 28g (Dietary Fiber 4g); Protein 3g **Carbohydrate Choices:** 2

**Tip** Pomegranate juices vary. Use pure pomegranate juice for the best flavor.

# Peachy White Tea Smoothies

**Prep Time:** 5 Minutes • **Start to Finish:** 30 Minutes • Makes 2 servings (1¼ cups each)

2 cups soymilk

8 bags peach-flavored white tea

3 cups frozen sliced peaches

¼ cup honey

**1** In 1-quart saucepan, heat soymilk just to boiling over medium-high heat, stirring constantly; remove from heat. Add tea bags and push into soymilk; let steep 5 minutes. Discard teabags. Place saucepan with soymilk mixture in freezer 15 to 20 minutes to chill.

**2** In blender or food processor, place chilled soymilk, peaches and honey. Cover; blend on high speed about 1 minute or until smooth.

**3** Pour into 2 glasses. Serve immediately.

**1 Serving:** Calories 330; Total Fat 3g (Saturated Fat 0.5g, Trans Fat 0g); Cholesterol 0mg; Sodium 200mg; Total Carbohydrate 68g (Dietary Fiber 5g); Protein 8g **Carbohydrate Choices:** 4½

**Tip** We like the peach-flavored tea in this delicious smoothie, but if you have unflavored white tea, go ahead and use it instead.

Satisfying Smoothies

# Creamy Mango Smoothies

**Prep Time:** 10 Minutes • **Start to Finish:** 10 Minutes • Makes 6 servings (1 cup each)

2 mangoes, seed removed, peeled and chopped (2 cups)

2 cups mango sorbet

2 containers (6 oz each) Yoplait Original 99% Fat Free French vanilla yogurt

1½ cups fat-free (skim) milk or soymilk

**1** In blender, place all ingredients. Cover; blend on high speed until smooth.

**2** Pour into 6 glasses. Serve immediately.

**1 Serving:** Calories 200; Total Fat 1g (Saturated Fat 0.5g, Trans Fat 0g); Cholesterol 0mg; Sodium 75mg; Total Carbohydrate 43g (Dietary Fiber 1g); Protein 5g **Carbohydrate Choices:** 3

**Tip** For the best flavor and color, choose ripe mangoes. Look for skins that are yellow with blushes of red.

# Peachy White Tea Smoothies

**Prep Time:** 5 Minutes • **Start to Finish:** 30 Minutes • Makes 2 servings (1¼ cups each)

2 cups soymilk

8 bags peach-flavored white tea

3 cups frozen sliced peaches

¼ cup honey

**1** In 1-quart saucepan, heat soymilk just to boiling over medium-high heat, stirring constantly; remove from heat. Add tea bags and push into soymilk; let steep 5 minutes. Discard teabags. Place saucepan with soymilk mixture in freezer 15 to 20 minutes to chill.

**2** In blender or food processor, place chilled soymilk, peaches and honey. Cover; blend on high speed about 1 minute or until smooth.

**3** Pour into 2 glasses. Serve immediately.

**1 Serving:** Calories 330; Total Fat 3g (Saturated Fat 0.5g, Trans Fat 0g); Cholesterol 0mg; Sodium 200mg; Total Carbohydrate 68g (Dietary Fiber 5g); Protein 8g **Carbohydrate Choices:** 4½

**Tip** We like the peach-flavored tea in this delicious smoothie, but if you have unflavored white tea, go ahead and use it instead.

# Creamy Mango Smoothies

**Prep Time:** 10 Minutes • **Start to Finish:** 10 Minutes • Makes 6 servings (1 cup each)

2 mangoes, seed removed, peeled and chopped (2 cups)

2 cups mango sorbet

2 containers (6 oz each) Yoplait Original 99% Fat Free French vanilla yogurt

1½ cups fat-free (skim) milk or soymilk

**1** In blender, place all ingredients. Cover; blend on high speed until smooth.

**2** Pour into 6 glasses. Serve immediately.

**1 Serving:** Calories 200; Total Fat 1g (Saturated Fat 0.5g, Trans Fat 0g); Cholesterol 0mg; Sodium 75mg; Total Carbohydrate 43g (Dietary Fiber 1g); Protein 5g **Carbohydrate Choices:** 3

**Tip** For the best flavor and color, choose ripe mangoes. Look for skins that are yellow with blushes of red.

# Obviously Orange Smoothies

**Prep Time:** 10 Minutes • **Start to Finish:** 10 Minutes • Makes 2 servings (1 cup each)

1 bag (12 oz) frozen broccoli cuts
1 cup frozen unsweetened mango chunks
½ cup carrot juice
½ cup orange juice
1 tablespoon sugar

**1** Cook broccoli as directed on bag. Rinse with cold water until cooled. Drain.

**2** In blender, place ¼ cup of the cooked broccoli and the remaining ingredients. (Cover and refrigerate remaining broccoli for another use.) Cover; blend on high speed about 30 seconds or until smooth.

**3** Pour into 2 glasses. Serve immediately.

**1 Serving:** Calories 140; Total Fat 0.5g (Saturated Fat 0g, Trans Fat 0g); Cholesterol 0mg; Sodium 20mg; Total Carbohydrate 32g (Dietary Fiber 2g); Protein 2g **Carbohydrate Choices:** 2

**Tip** Look for the carrot juice in the refrigerated case of the produce section.

# Super-Athlete Spinach Smoothies

**Prep Time:** 10 Minutes • **Start to Finish:** 10 Minutes • Makes 2 servings (1 cup each)

1 box (9 oz) frozen chopped spinach
1 container (6 oz) Yoplait Greek Fat Free blueberry yogurt
1 avocado half, pitted, peeled
¾ cup cranberry-blueberry juice
½ cup frozen blueberries

**1** Microwave spinach as directed on box. Rinse with cold water until cooled. Drain, squeezing out as much liquid as possible.

**2** In blender, place ¼ cup of the cooked spinach and the remaining ingredients. (Cover and refrigerate remaining spinach for another use.) Cover; blend on high speed about 30 seconds or until smooth.

**3** Pour into 2 glasses. Serve immediately.

**1 Serving:** Calories 230; Total Fat 6g (Saturated Fat 1g, Trans Fat 0g); Cholesterol 5mg; Sodium 75mg; Total Carbohydrate 36g (Dietary Fiber 5g); Protein 8g **Carbohydrate Choices:** 2½

**Tip** Here's an easy way to pit an avocado: Cut the avocado lengthwise in half around the pit, and pull apart the halves. The pit will stay in one of the halves. Firmly and carefully strike the pit with the sharp edge of a knife. While holding the avocado, twist the knife to loosen and remove the pit.

## Party Cocktails

# Strawberry–Hard Lemonade Slush

**Prep Time:** 15 Minutes • **Start to Finish:** 4 Hours 15 Minutes • Makes 23 servings (¾ cup each)

1 box (4-serving size) strawberry-flavored gelatin

1 cup boiling water

2 boxes (10 oz each) frozen strawberries in light syrup, partially thawed

1 quart (4 cups) fresh strawberries, hulled

1 can (12 oz) frozen lemonade concentrate, partially thawed

½ cup sugar

1 bottle (11.2 oz) hard lemonade 5% alcohol beverage or 1 can (12 oz) lemon-lime carbonated beverage

6 additional bottles (11.2 oz each) hard lemonade 5% alcohol beverage or 1 bottle (2 liters) lemon-lime carbonated beverage or ginger ale, chilled

**1** In 13 x 9-inch (3-quart) glass baking dish, place gelatin. Pour boiling water on gelatin; stir until gelatin is dissolved.

**2** In food processor, place strawberries in syrup, fresh strawberries, lemonade concentrate and sugar. Cover; process until smooth. Pour into gelatin. Stir in 1 bottle hard lemonade. Freeze at least 4 hours or overnight until slush consistency, stirring after 2 hours.

**3** Spoon ½ cup slush mixture into each glass. Pour ⅓ cup hard lemonade over each. Stir and serve.

**1 Serving:** Calories 160; Total Fat 0g (Saturated Fat 0g, Trans Fat 0g); Cholesterol 0mg; Sodium 20mg; Total Carbohydrate 31g (Dietary Fiber 1g); Protein 0g **Carbohydrate Choices:** 2

**Tip** If you don't own a food processor, use a blender to blend the ingredients in batches.

# Blueberry Hard Lemonade

**Prep Time:** 10 Minutes • **Start to Finish:** 10 Minutes • Makes 1 serving

- 2 tablespoons fresh blueberries
- 1 tablespoon fresh lemon juice
- 2 fresh mint leaves
- Ice cubes
- 2 tablespoons gin
- ½ cup ginger ale or lemon-lime soda
- Lemon wedge and blueberries on a beverage pick with fresh mint, if desired

**1** In a highball glass, muddle blueberries, lemon juice and mint.

**2** Fill glass to rim with ice cubes. Add gin. Top with ginger ale; stir gently.

**3** Garnish as desired.

**1 Serving:** Calories 130; Total Fat 0g (Saturated Fat 0g, Trans Fat 0g); Cholesterol 0mg; Sodium 10mg; Total Carbohydrate 16g (Dietary Fiber 0g); Protein 0g **Carbohydrate Choices:** 1

**Tip** What does "muddle" mean? When mixing cocktails, herbs and/or fruit are often mashed or ground — muddled — in the bottom of a glass before adding the liquid ingredients to intensify their flavors. You can muddle with a spoon or a pestle-like tool called a muddler.

# White Wine Sangria

**Prep Time:** 10 Minutes • **Start to Finish:** 10 Minutes • Makes 12 servings

½ cup sugar

1 cup orange-flavored liqueur or orange juice

1 cup vodka or lemon-lime carbonated beverage

2 medium peaches or nectarines, thinly sliced, slices cut in half

1 medium orange, thinly sliced, cut in half if desired

1 lemon, thinly sliced

1 lime, thinly sliced

1 bottle (750 ml) dry white wine, nonalcoholic white wine or white grape juice, chilled (3½ cups)

1 bottle (1 liter) club soda, chilled (4 cups)

**1** In half-gallon glass or plastic pitcher, stir sugar, orange liqueur and vodka until sugar is dissolved.

**2** Into another half-gallon glass or plastic pitcher, pour half of vodka mixture. Divide fruits and wine evenly between pitchers.

**3** Just before serving, pour half of club soda into each pitcher; stir gently to mix. Serve immediately. If desired, serve over ice.

**1 Serving:** Calories 200; Total Fat 0g (Saturated Fat 0g, Trans Fat 0g); Cholesterol 0mg; Sodium 20mg; Total Carbohydrate 20g (Dietary Fiber 0g); Protein 0g **Carbohydrate Choices:** 1

**Tip** The nice thing about this fruity, refreshing drink is that inexpensive liqueur, vodka and wine can be used because the flavor doesn't rely solely upon alcohol. Try Triple Sec for the orange liqueur and a Chablis Blanc or Chardonnay for the dry white wine.

# Skinny Clementine Martini

**Prep Time:** 10 Minutes • **Start to Finish:** 10 Minutes • Makes 1 serving

2 tablespoons gin or citrus-flavored vodka

1 tablespoon elderflower liqueur or orange-flavored liqueur

3 tablespoons fresh clementine juice, fresh pink grapefruit juice or pomegranate juice

1 tablespoon fresh lime juice

Ice cubes

2 tablespoons club soda

Clementine slice, pink grapefruit peel twist or fresh lime slice for garnish

Add some clever sparkle to your next party. Enjoy these natural, light martinis made with fresh juice, high-quality liquor and a splash of club soda. Lower-calorie cocktails never tasted, or looked, so sweet. Cheers!

**1** Pour gin, liqueur and juices into shaker with ice; shake until well mixed. Pour into chilled martini glass, straining out ice. Top off with club soda. Garnish with clementine slice.

**1 Serving:** Calories 130; Total Fat 0g (Saturated Fat 0g, Trans Fat 0g); Cholesterol 0mg; Sodium 10mg; Total Carbohydrate 10g (Dietary Fiber 0g); Protein 0g **Carbohydrate Choices:** ½

**Tip** Fresh fruit juice is the secret to making these refreshing skinny cocktails. Try all three variations — clementine, pink grapefruit and pomegranate.

# Thai Basil Mojitarita

**Prep Time:** 5 Minutes • **Start to Finish:** 5 Minutes • Makes 1 serving

2 teaspoons light agave nectar
1 tablespoon fresh lime juice
4 fresh Thai basil leaves
2 tablespoons blanco tequila
Ice cubes
4 tablespoons club soda, chilled
Lime wedge and additional basil leaves, if desired

**1** Pour agave nectar and lime juice into highball glass. Add basil leaves; gently break up basil with muddler or spoon.

**2** Add tequila; fill glass with ice.

**3** Top with club soda; stir gently. Garnish with lime wedge and basil leaf.

**1 Serving:** Calories 120; Total Fat 0g (Saturated Fat 0g, Trans Fat 0g); Cholesterol 0mg; Sodium 15mg; Total Carbohydrate 13g (Dietary Fiber 0g); Protein 0g **Carbohydrate Choices:** 1

**Tip** If you can't find Thai basil, substitute fresh mint.

# Beergaritas

**Prep Time:** 10 Minutes • **Start to Finish:** 10 Minutes • Makes 8 servings

1 can (12 oz) frozen limeade concentrate, thawed

1 cup tequila

¼ cup orange-flavored liqueur

2 bottles (12 oz each) light-colored beer

Crushed ice

8 lime slices

**1** In large pitcher, mix limeade concentrate, tequila and liqueur until well blended. Pour beer into pitcher; stir.

**2** Fill 8 lowball or margarita glasses with crushed ice. Pour beer mixture over ice. Garnish each with lime slice.

**1 Serving:** Calories 210; Total Fat 0g (Saturated Fat 0g, Trans Fat 0g); Cholesterol 0mg; Sodium 0mg; Total Carbohydrate 31g (Dietary Fiber 0g); Protein 0g **Carbohydrate Choices:** 2

**Tip** For an authentic touch, salt the rims of the glasses. Pour ½ cup coarse (kosher or sea) salt onto a small flat plate. Rub a lime wedge around the rim of each glass and then dip it into the salt.

# Mango Margaritas

**Prep Time:** 10 Minutes • **Start to Finish:** 10 Minutes • Makes 4 servings

2 to 3 limes

¼ cup coarse (kosher or sea) salt

Crushed ice

1½ cups mango juice drink from concentrate (35% juice)

1 cup tequila

½ cup orange-flavored liqueur

**1** Cut 4 thin slices from 1 lime; set aside. Cut 1 small wedge from same lime. Squeeze remaining limes to get ¼ cup juice; set aside.

**2** Rub lime wedge around rim of each of 4 margarita glasses. Pour salt onto small flat plate; dip rim of each glass into salt. Fill glasses with crushed ice.

**3** In 4-cup glass measuring cup, mix mango juice, tequila, liqueur and reserved ¼ cup lime juice. Pour mixture over ice in glasses. Garnish each with lime slice.

**1 Serving:** Calories 280; Total Fat 0g (Saturated Fat 0g, Trans Fat 0g); Cholesterol 0mg; Sodium 3370mg; Total Carbohydrate 25g (Dietary Fiber 1g); Protein 0g **Carbohydrate Choices:** 1½

**Tip** For a special touch and sweeter taste, substitute 2 tablespoons granulated sugar for half of the coarse salt for rimming the glasses.

# Metric Conversion Guide

## Volume

| U.S. Units | Canadian Metric | Australian Metric |
|---|---|---|
| ¼ teaspoon | 1 mL | 1 ml |
| ½ teaspoon | 2 mL | 2 ml |
| 1 teaspoon | 5 mL | 5 ml |
| 1 tablespoon | 15 mL | 20 ml |
| ¼ cup | 50 mL | 60 ml |
| ⅓ cup | 75 mL | 80 ml |
| ½ cup | 125 mL | 125 ml |
| ⅔ cup | 150 mL | 170 ml |
| ¾ cup | 175 mL | 190 ml |
| 1 cup | 250 mL | 250 ml |
| 1 quart | 1 liter | 1 liter |
| 1½ quarts | 1.5 liters | 1.5 liters |
| 2 quarts | 2 liters | 2 liters |
| 2½ quarts | 2.5 liters | 2.5 liters |
| 3 quarts | 3 liters | 3 liters |
| 4 quarts | 4 liters | 4 liters |

## Weight

| U.S. Units | Canadian Metric | Australian Metric |
|---|---|---|
| 1 ounce | 30 grams | 30 grams |
| 2 ounces | 55 grams | 60 grams |
| 3 ounces | 85 grams | 90 grams |
| 4 ounces (¼ pound) | 115 grams | 125 grams |
| 8 ounces (½ pound) | 225 grams | 225 grams |
| 16 ounces (1 pound) | 455 grams | 500 grams |
| 1 pound | 455 grams | 0.5 kilogram |

Note: The recipes in this cookbook have not been developed or tested using metric measures. When converting recipes to metric, some variations in quality may be noted.

## Measurements

| Inches | Centimeters |
|---|---|
| 1 | 2.5 |
| 2 | 5.0 |
| 3 | 7.5 |
| 4 | 10.0 |
| 5 | 12.5 |
| 6 | 15.0 |
| 7 | 17.5 |
| 8 | 20.5 |
| 9 | 23.0 |
| 10 | 25.5 |
| 11 | 28.0 |
| 12 | 30.5 |
| 13 | 33.0 |

## Temperatures

| Fahrenheit | Celsius |
|---|---|
| 32° | 0° |
| 212° | 100° |
| 250° | 120° |
| 275° | 140° |
| 300° | 150° |
| 325° | 160° |
| 350° | 180° |
| 375° | 190° |
| 400° | 200° |
| 425° | 220° |
| 450° | 230° |
| 475° | 240° |
| 500° | 260° |

# Recipe Testing and Calculating Nutrition Information

## Recipe Testing:

- Large eggs and 2% milk were used unless otherwise indicated.
- Fat-free, low-fat, low-sodium or lite products were not used unless indicated.
- No nonstick cookware and bakeware were used unless otherwise indicated. No dark-colored, black or insulated bakeware was used.
- When a pan is specified, a metal pan was used; a baking dish or pie plate means ovenproof glass was used.
- An electric hand mixer was used for mixing only when mixer speeds are specified.

## Calculating Nutrition:

- The first ingredient was used wherever a choice is given, such as ⅓ cup sour cream or plain yogurt.
- The first amount was used wherever a range is given, such as 3- to 3½-pound whole chicken.
- The first serving number was used wherever a range is given, such as 4 to 6 servings.
- "If desired" ingredients were not included.
- Only the amount of a marinade or frying oil that is absorbed was included.

# America's most trusted cookbook is better than ever!

- 1,100 all-new photos, including hundreds of step-by-step images
- More than 1,500 recipes, with hundreds of inspiring variations and creative "mini" recipes for easy cooking ideas
- Brand-new features
- Gorgeous new design

**Get the best edition of the *Betty Crocker Cookbook* today!**

www.ingramcontent.com/pod-product-compliance
Lightning Source LLC
Chambersburg PA
CBHW071418290426
44108CB00014B/1883